THE
UNITED STATES
AND GERMANY

The Elihu Root Lectures

The Elihu Root Lectures, inaugurated in 1958, were named for a founder of the Council on Foreign Relations, who was its Honorary President from 1921 to 1937. Elihu Root served as Secretary of War (1899–1904), Secretary of State (1905–1909), United States Senator (1909–1915), and remained an influential "elder statesman" until his death in 1937.

The Root Lectures are given periodically and provide an opportunity for a distinguished Council member to reflect on his or her experience in public life and to address a major foreign policy issue from the perspective of that experience. The first Root Lectures were given by Thomas K. Finletter. Subsequent Root Lecturers were Dean Rusk, Caryl Haskins, Edward S. Mason, George Kennan, Robert Roosa, James Reston, Francis T. Plimpton, George W. Ball, Harvey Brooks, Carroll Wilson, J. William Fulbright, Jacob Javits, and Lewis Thomas.

THE
UNITED STATES
AND GERMANY

A VITAL PARTNERSHIP

The Elihu Root Lectures
February 1986

ARTHUR F. BURNS
Foreword by Helmut Schmidt

Council on Foreign Relations

COUNCIL ON FOREIGN RELATIONS BOOKS

Copyright © 1986 by the Council on Foreign Relations, Inc.
All rights reserved.
Printed in the United States of America.

Library of Congress Cataloging- in-Publication Data

Burns, Arthur F. (Arthur Frank), 1904–
  The United States and Germany.

  (The Elihu Root Lectures ; Feb. 1986)
  1. United States—Foreign relations—Germany (West)
2. Germany (West)—Foreign relations—United States. I. Council
on Foreign Relations. II. Title. III. Series: Elihu Root lectures ; 1986.
E183.8.G3B79   1986   327.73043   86-8821
ISBN 0-87609-018-8

Contents

Foreword

In an age of telecommunications and of a tight network of airlines covering a shrinking globe there are people who believe that Ambassadors fit into the modern picture somewhat as dinosaurs would look on Times Square. But whoever has had the opportunity during his or her political life to meet one of the small number of truly outstanding diplomats will know that no technical instrument will ever supersede the crucial impact that personality can have on the whole fabric of political and human ties between nations.

One will not be surprised that I count Ambassador Burns among this very small set of genuine representatives of their nation who at the same time have become sincere interpreters on behalf of their host nation. Dialogues between nations do at times tend to be burdened by many languages. It takes understanding, prudence and tact to overcome the difficulties. If one adds knowledge, judgment, honesty, and—if necessary—also courage (with these qualities applied in both directions between host and home governments), then we have the definition of a great diplomat. And at the same time a definition of Arthur Burns.

Our acquaintance dates from July 1972 when I, as newly installed Federal Minister of Economy and Finance, paid my first visit—together with George Shultz, then Secretary of the Treasury—to Fed-Chairman Arthur Burns. He was our senior

by one and a half decades, and so we behaved respectfully—
Shultz because he knew Arthur Burns, and I because an authority like Karl Klasen, then President of the Bundesbank,
had expressed to me his high esteem for the Fed-Chief. It was
a time of great upheavals in the international monetary system which only nine months later resulted in the breakdown
of the Bretton Woods system of fixed exchange rates. We
Europeans at that time still hoped for a chance to keep the system alive and working. I had learned from my elder friend
Alex Moeller that international monetary policy is a constitu-
tive element of economic policy as well as of foreign policy. So
our conversations with the Fed-Chief in summer 1972 were
bound to become very serious indeed. I will never forget one
of Arthur Burns' side remarks: "You talk a lot of sense, young
man." Although I was already 53 years old, I have tried to live
up to this standard ever after.

When in 1981 President Reagan decided to send Arthur
Burns as his Ambassador to Bonn, he took a very political decision by appointing a man whose personal friendship with
the Federal Chancellor of those days was well known. It gave
credit to Arthur Burns that his role in the political as in the
public life of his host country was by no means harmed when
late in 1982 a new party coalition and a new Chancellor came
into office and the German personnel was changed.

James "Scotty" Reston, dean of American political jour-
nalism, was probably right in saying that Ambassador Burns'
success story in Bonn was largely due to the fact that he had
contacts with everyone, but didn't chime in with anyone—not
even his colleagues in the White House or the Treasury.

Indeed, Arthur Burns—and this volume gives ample
proof of this—has spoken and does speak, detached from
daily political struggles, in a broader historical perspective;
and he does this with a masterful eloquence. As he once put it:
in cases of differing opinions it is not crucial who in the end
will "win" or who will "lose," but it remains decisive whether

both have tried to move closer together and to understand each other's interests.

Arthur Burns has an excellent understanding of German interests and has pleaded for them in Washington as impressively as he did for American interests in Bonn. He appealed to the conscience of my compatriots, but at the same time he encouraged us to take pride in our history and faith in the future of our divided nation. He represented us in Washington as a dependable friend. He explained to his countrymen the anxieties among some of our young people. He pointed time and again to the fact that the best support for our common defense does consist in concentrating on our common political, cultural and economic values. Whoever has ears to hear in Washington or Bonn should listen.

For a son of a Jewish family from Austro-Hungarian Galicia who became a citizen of the United States as a child, it was by no means natural to become a friend of the German people. But Arthur Burns is above aversion or hatred. He pleads for mutual understanding, not for forgetting. It is a man of reconciliation whom I now picture sitting at his desk in the small wooden cottage a hundred yards away from his old farmhouse in Vermont, reading, writing, and smoking his indispensable pipe. Whatever comes from that desk should be read in the United States, for a great nation needs advice and enlightenment to stay great. And it also ought to be read in Germany—in remembrance of a true friend and at the same time of a man of outstanding judgment, and therefore not only with gratitude but also with curiosity and attention.

Helmut Schmidt

Preface

When I was invited by our government in the spring of 1981 to become Ambassador to the Federal Republic of Germany, I was pleased and felt honored; but I needed time to ponder my decision. There were reasons for hesitation. While enjoying good health, I was already seventy-seven years old. My entire professional life had been devoted to economics and finance. I was still involved in national debates on economic policy, besides working on a book on the problem of inflation. Moreover, my familiarity with the political aspects of foreign affairs was at best spotty, and my knowledge of the art of diplomacy was practically nil.

The opportunity of going to Bonn nevertheless had its appeal. I had long had an interest in Germany, having visited there many times either in a personal or a governmental capacity. I still remembered a little of the German language and literature from my student days. I knew a fair number of business, financial, and political leaders in the Federal Republic. The redoubtable Helmut Schmidt, then the German Chancellor, was an old friend. The prospect of embarking on a new career that offered the possibility of contributing to the preservation of peace and freedom in our troubled world stirred my imagination. And being a practicing Jew, I vaguely felt that there might be a certain moral fitness, perhaps a step toward further reconciliation, in becoming ambassador to a country that had perpetrated during the Nazi era unspeakable crimes against my co-religionists, including members of my own family. In the end, I chose to go to Bonn, and I have never had the slightest doubt about the rightness of that decision.

The Elihu Root Lectures, which I delivered during February of this year, gave me the opportunity to present some reflections on my mission in Germany. In preparing the lectures, I have benefited from the stimulating counsel of several friends—John C. Kornblum, Nelson C. Ledsky, Hans N. Tuch, and William M. Woessner, with whom I had the privilege of working during my ambassadorship in Germany, as well as from Arthur L. Broida, Jean Balestrieri, and Laurence M. Band, my present associates at the American Enterprise Institute. I am also grateful to Paul Kreisberg and his colleagues at the Council on Foreign Relations for their kind assistance in preparing the lectures for the printer.

Arthur F. Burns

March 5, 1986

ONE

What I Learned in Germany

In considering what I might best discuss in the first of these Elihu Root Lectures, I pondered the various issues in which I was involved as our country's Ambassador to the Federal Republic of Germany. I finally decided to devote this lecture mainly to my impressions of Germany and its people and to leave the more specific concerns of our nation's foreign policy to the later lectures. Accordingly, my remarks today will be focused on what I experienced and learned during my four years of living and working in that remarkable country.

Concept of Ambassadorship

One thing that I learned quickly is that problems of foreign policy are vastly harder to define and deal with than the problems of economics on which I had hitherto worked. The field of economics nowadays abounds in facts and figures—many of them widely known and of a high degree of accuracy. To be sure, specific problems—such as youth unemployment, inflation, or the plight of farmers or bankers—raise difficult questions of diagnosis and still more difficult questions of how they can be resolved. As everyone knows, ways of coping with economic issues lead frequently to controversy, but the elements involved in public debates—

whether they stem from differences of diagnosis or ideology—can ordinarily still be defined with some precision. Economic issues, both domestic and international, were to me, therefore, a territory of relative order and predictability. International politics and diplomacy, on the other hand, were a quite new discipline. I found it at the very start, and in fact still do, a universe inordinately filled with gossip, emotion, even distrust and suspicion—a world in which perceptions of reality often obscure the facts themselves.

This realization troubled me, and yet it need not have done so. After all, understanding among governments depends on human beings, and human understanding is never perfect. That this is man's lot on earth is evident from our daily lives. Parents do not always understand their children, or children their parents. So it is also between husbands and wives, between employers and their workmen, between bankers and borrowers, between landlords and tenants, between professors and students. But if misunderstandings exist within our families, schools, and workshops, they have much greater opportunity to arise—and even flourish—among nations, where differences of history, language, and geography often conspire with limited direct contacts between peoples to breed confusion and at times, unfortunately, even mistrust. While foreign affairs are no longer a new interest for me, I continue to be astounded by the strange opinions that highly placed Americans now and then express about Germany or its people and their governmental leaders. I need hardly add that influential Germans are occasionally just as reckless in characterizing our country and its leadership.

Feeling, as I often did, that I was working in a modern Tower of Babel, I concluded soon after coming to Bonn that my Embassy must concentrate on clearing away the underbrush of emotion and faulty perception that now and then disturbed the relationship between the United States and the country to which I was accredited. In my meetings with members of the Embassy staff, I therefore kept stressing the need to respect the boundary line between sheer opinion and true knowledge—the importance of eschewing the titillations of gossip, of verifying rumors wherever possible. Our task was to focus on matters that seriously concerned American interests, and we were to do that without meddling in the domestic politics of our host country.

I naturally joined my able staff in this endeavor, and I did not confine myself to Bonn politicians and civil servants. In extensive travels across West Germany I met with businessmen, journalists, members of the clergy, school and university teachers, factory workers and their leaders. Of special interest to me were the young people, particularly university students, whom I often invited to join me in seminars. As a former professor, the attitudes of young people toward their own society and our America were of intrinsic interest to me. Beyond that, since many of today's students were destined to become in a not-distant future their country's leaders in business, education, and government, I deemed it an important part of my ambassadorial duties to become acquainted with their thinking and perhaps even help a few in finding their way to a constructive future.

The young people of Germany won my heart. As a group, they are lively, courteous, intelligent, free of guile, idealistic. I found them striving against great odds to find their identity in a divided nation. I found them seriously concerned about the future of their country. Most of them were only vaguely aware of the excesses of Soviet communism. They were perplexed about social policies in the United States or the wisdom of our government. What came through to me most clearly was their fear that the armaments race between the two superpowers might devastate their country.

It was easy to like these youngsters and to sympathize with their general mood and concerns. At the same time, I was troubled by some of their distorted views concerning the United States, and perhaps even more by their lack of familiarity with European or their own country's history. Relatively few knew about the Marshall Plan or the Baruch Plan, or how the freedom of Berlin had been preserved by a massive Western airlift, or what happened in Hungary in 1956 or in Czechoslovakia in 1968, or even about the role of their parents and grandparents in establishing a viable democracy and rebuilding their devastated country after the Second World War.

Some of the students I encountered—a minority, to be sure, but not an insignificant minority—saw little or no moral difference between American and Soviet conduct, either domestically or internationally. In addressing adult audiences in Germany, I therefore frequently commented on the lack of historical perspective of German youth. When told, as happened at times, that Russian propaganda was to blame, I could not avoid observing that it was the responsibility of parents and teachers to foster a sense of history in children, that historical teaching had apparently been neglected in German homes and schools, and that the Soviets—to the extent that they had any part in this at all—simply took advantage of the opportunities offered by the inadequacy of historical education within Germany.

German vs. American
Foreign Policy Interests

But if German youngsters had much to learn about their country's history and its place in the world, so too did I. I knew, of course, that the Federal Repubic was a loyal member of NATO and that it made substantial contributions to NATO's effectiveness. The constraints of German foreign policy, however, were unknown to me when I arrived in Bonn. In time, it became clear to me that while Americans and Germans share fundamental political, military, and economic interests, they still brought different perspectives to world problems.

The United States, having become a world power in the past forty years, brings a global view to international affairs. German interests, on the other hand, are mainly regional. A nation located in the heart of Europe, having lost a large portion of its prewar territory to the Soviet Union and Poland, being troubled over the fate of still another portion that became a separate German state under Soviet domination, could hardly be expected to show great boldness in foreign affairs with any frequency. With Soviet troops and missiles concentrated on its shrunken borders, West Germany could not readily join the United States every time we reacted to Soviet threats around the world. In this age of nuclear weaponry, American cities—Seattle, Chicago, New York—are no less vulnerable to atomic destruction than are Hamburg, Frankfurt, or Munich. Americans, however, do not feel Russians breathing down their necks as Germans do. It may seem obvious to Americans that when we, for example, take military steps to protect Western interests in the Persian Gulf, our NATO allies, whose dependence on Arab oil is much greater than ours, should fully support us. The Germans, along with other Europeans, however, do not feel powerful enough to run significant risks in that direction. We may deplore their hesitation and try to overcome it, but realism requires that we understand it.

I learned also other reasons why Germans see East-West relations somewhat differently from most Americans. If one asked a typical citizen of the Federal Republic to list the benefits of détente, he could point to normalization in and around Berlin, to improved personal contacts between the citizens of the two Germanys, to the return of several hundred thousand ethnic Germans from Eastern Europe in recent years, to stronger economic ties between Western and Eastern Europe—in short, to a whole range of developments that can be attributed to the flowering of détente in the 1970s. On the other hand, a typical American citizen, if asked to identify how détente has affected his life, would be hard put to respond. From a purely domestic standpoint, it is not easy for Americans to come up with a telling argument for détente. And when we turn to the international scene, we cannot avoid feeling that our expectations from the policy of détente have been disappointed—that repression of human rights has not diminished in the Soviet Union, while its military buildup and adventurism around the world have actually increased since the early 1970s.

Besides sensing the different perceptions concerning détente and about the role of our NATO allies outside of Europe, I came to understand that Germany's membership in the European Community involved political and moral obligations that occasionally made it difficult, even when the German government saw practically eye to eye with ours, to give strong public support to American initiatives. Partnership with the United States is vitally important to Germany, and most Germans know it; but so also is cooperation with other members of the Community—most of all, with France.

The dream of a United States of Europe, which seemed close to realization in the aftermath of war, has dimmed with the passage of time. Young people, many of whom were eager right after the war to embrace the ideal of a united Europe, seem to have lost faith in a European Community that squanders so much of its energy in tiresome debates over budgets and agricultural prices. However, the goal of a politically united Western Europe, while no longer being pushed energetically, is still alive among a fair number of German intellectuals and politicians. And in any event, effective cooperation between Germany and other members of the European Community has become essential to Germany's political as well as its economic future.

My realization that German perceptions and interests diverged in some significant respects from ours led me to conclusions which, while perhaps obvious, are not always respected. First, the basic task of international diplomacy is to be aware of divergent perceptions and to accommodate divergent national interests. Second, this essential objective requires patience and is best pursued without the fanfare of publicity. Third, there need not be winners or losers in international disputes. Every country has its pride, and it is therefore the better part of wisdom that a winner, if indeed there be one, celebrate victory by silence. Fourth, more effective consultative procedures among the nations of NATO are needed in the interest of harmony within the Alliance. Although meetings among members of the foreign policy and defense establishments of NATO occur rather frequently, they have not been thorough enough or timely enough—perhaps not even frequent enough—to avoid occasional serious misunderstandings.

Imperfect communication can lead to severe strains among allies. Let me give an example. Upon arriving in Bonn, I already knew that our government was unhappy about a European project to finance the construction of a pipeline from Siberia and to enter into contracts with the Soviets for acquiring natural gas once the pipeline was completed. Our government feared that as a result of the pipeline several of the countries in Western Europe, especially Germany, would become dependent on Soviet supplies and thus run the risk of becoming easy targets for political blackmail. To ward off such a dangerous development, our government undertook to work out an alternative plan for meeting Europe's energy needs, but we never offered a practical alternative. This troubled European governments, since they had become convinced that assuring an adequate supply of natural gas was essential to their future and that Russian supplies, even if politically manipulated, could not cause any significant industrial dislocation.

After long delays the German government finally informed us that it had decided to go ahead with the Siberian pipeline. Our government was reluctant to drop the issue and still kept pressing the Germans and other Europeans to give up the project. With German officials becoming increasingly irritated, I was bluntly told one day by the German Minister of Economics that the American government did not seem to realize that the Federal Republic of Germany is a sovereign country, that its decision to go ahead with the pipeline—whether right or wrong, wise or unwise—was irrevocable, and that the German government would appreciate our finally grasping this fact. I, of course, saw to it that the authorities in Washington were fully informed about German sentiments. Nevertheless, feelings on the pipeline project continued to run strong in our capital. Delegations were still sent to Bonn to try to convince the Germans to drop the project. And to make matters worse, as an aftermath of Poland's decision to outlaw Solidarity, our government decreed that supplies needed to build the pipeline could not be shipped even by European subsidiaries or licensees of American firms.

This assertion of extraterritorial rights infuriated the business community and officialdom in Germany—also in France, Britain, and Italy. For a time it appeared that the Polish crisis was turning into a crisis of the Alliance, and indeed it took all of Secretary Shultz's unique skill in the art of negotiation to give a constructive turn to the smoldering pipeline dispute. In the end, European interests were accommodated; but European governments also understood more clearly than before that the interests of the Alliance called for great caution in putting resources at the disposal of the Soviets that could strengthen their already formidable military establishment. I need hardly add that if consultations between our government and the Europeans had been more thorough, this unhappy dispute could have been avoided.

German Economic Difficulties

The extensive unemployment that existed then in Germany and throughout Western Europe of course contributed to the intensity of feelings about the pipeline project. But, as I gradually learned through close attention to developments in the European economy, Germany's difficulties during the early 1980s did not stem merely from the international business recession. In fact, they were superimposed on a protracted loss of economic dynamism—a weakening of underlying forces of economic growth that had once led the world to look upon Germany as a land of economic miracles.

My first visit to Europe occurred in 1950 when I had a sabbatical from my university. After spending some months in Britain, France, and Switzerland, I moved on to Germany. The first night there was sleepless, thanks to a construction crew working on the road outside my hotel in Frankfurt. After resting most of the next day, my wife and I took a walk along one of the main thoroughfares of that busy city. The most impressive—indeed a truly astonishing—sight was that of masons laying brick under electric lights at nine and ten o'clock at night. Upon returning to the States, when business friends sought my impressions of the European economy, I answered without hesitation: "Within a very few years Germany will once again be the strongest industrial power in Europe." To surprised inquirers who sought my reasons, I simply replied: "In contrast to most of Europe, the Germans really work."

This I cannot say any longer. To be sure, the economy of West Germany is still the strongest in Europe. Much of German science, research, and technology is highly regarded everywhere; but Germans no longer work the way they did in the years immediately after the war. The workweek has become shorter; holidays have increased in number; long vacations have become practically universal; sick leaves and rest cures have multiplied; early retirements have become more frequent; and generous governmental benefits for unemployed workers have helped to swell their ranks. Nor is this work-reducing process yet at an end. Two years ago, the metal workers' union subjected the German economy to a costly strike, insisting on a reduction of the standard workweek from 40 to 35 hours at an unchanged weekly wage. Although the strike was hardly popular with the German people, it did have the public support of one of the major political parties. The strike was finally settled by reducing the average workweek by an hour and a half.

During the past two to three years, Germany along with the rest of Western Europe has experienced economic recovery, but the recovery has been stronger in Germany than elsewhere, it has nevertheless been of moderate scope and as yet has not led to a perceptible reduction of unemployment. The loss of economic dynamism in Western Europe has many causes, but I have come to believe that the most important of them is the explosive growth of welfare programs since 1970. This has undoubtedly contributed to social tranquility, but the economic cost has been heavy. In Germany, as in Western Europe taken as a whole, government spending now constitutes about 50 percent of the gross national product. This flowering of the welfare state has generally led to higher taxes, more rigid labor markets, rising labor costs, extensive government regulation, and a weaker trend in profits. Bureaucratic obstacles that impede the private sector now cover the European economic landscape. The recent economic recovery has indeed brought a substantial expansion of German exports and an improvement in profits; incentives for undertaking large business capital investments nevertheless are still inadequate. When Chancellor Kohl assumed office in 1982, it was widely expected that the burden of taxes and government regulation would soon be substantially lightened; but these hopes have so far been fulfilled only to a limited degree.

The strength of the American economy is widely admired in Germany. Uneasiness exists, however, about the vicissitudes of our business cycle, and the thrust of our governmental economic policies. Once it became evident toward the end of 1984 that the rapid pace of economic expansion in the United States was no longer continuing, many German businessmen and government officials became seriously concerned about the consequences of the American slowdown for their nation's economy. The prevailing sentiment seemed to be that, taken in the aggregate, business in Germany echoed, so to speak, business conditions in the United States; that what happened in the German economy was to a large degree a passive response to developments in the American economy; and that the United States was not giving sufficient attention to the consequences of its policies—particularly with regard to government finances, interest rates, and exchange rates—for other countries.

This feeling of dependence on the United States is by no means confined to Germany. Moral philosophers may deplore such an attitude, and economists may consider it exaggerated, but there is no denying that it is widespread. European business psychology has deep roots in economic experience during the immediate postwar years when Europe was in shambles, and this feeling of inadequacy is sustained by Western Europe's continuing dependence on the United States for protection against the Soviet military threat.

Feelings of self-reliance normally bring confidence and foster hope, and are no less important in the life of a nation than in the life of an individual. Such feelings are nowadays stronger in Germany and elsewhere in Western Europe than in the late 1940s or 1950s, but they are not yet robust enough to match American attitudes. A majority of Germans admire the venturesome spirit of American business firms, like Americans, and appreciate our military umbrella; but their appreciation is at times tinged with resentment—not a surprising attitude among people who are burdened with a sense of dependence.

Criticism of American economic and cultural institutions and of our political leadership is voiced frequently in Germany, especially by students, teachers, clergymen, and politicians outside the governing coalition. But I have encountered very little overt anti-Americanism—at least if one interprets that to mean hostility or hatred toward our country. And to the extent that such sentiment exists in Germany, it must not be identified with pro-Sovietism. There are Germans, quite understandably, who are anti-American and anti-Soviet at the same time.

Echoes of the Nazi Era

Germans, like most people in the world, tend to be ethnocentric. The presence of several million "guest workers" in Germany seems, however, to have fostered greater tolerance of other ethnic groups—except perhaps for the Turks, who, I regret to say, appear to be viewed with a touch of contempt even by many highly educated men and women. Anti-semitism has not vanished, but its virulent expression is now confined to a tiny minority. Most Germans are well aware of Nazi crimes against the Jewish people, and are truly remorseful. I found them sensitively attentive to their Jewish compatriots and generally supportive of the state of Israel. It was nevertheless of interest to me to hear German admirers of Judaism refer to the vital importance of German-Jewish friendship rather than to Christian-Jewish friendship. They were obviously unaware of the discriminatory implication of their phrasing.

The Bitburg affair, of which much was heard on both sides of the Atlantic in April and May 1985, came toward the end of my sojourn in Germany. As some of you may recall, May 8 marked the fortieth anniversary of the end of World War II in Europe. To Americans it was a time for commemorating the victory of the Allies, the end of Nazi tyranny, and the rebirth of freedom in Western Europe. The citizens of West Germany, however, inevitably had ambivalent feelings about the occasion. The end of bombings and the restoration of their freedom were indeed cause for rejoicing; but May 8 also evoked memories of military defeat, the dismemberment of their country, and the replacement of Nazi tyranny by Soviet oppression of many millions of their brethren in the Russian zone. This was a time when the spiritual need of the German people was to be by themselves; it was a time to recall and come to terms with the past, a time for meditation, a time for prayer, a time for rededication to democracy, tolerance, and international good will. Eager though the German people might have been for a visit by the American President, early May was hardly the best time for it. But it so happened that the German government had invited President Reagan; he had graciously accepted, and the German Chancellery and the White House were proceeding with plans for the visit.

Despite the sensitivity of the season, everything would probably have gone smoothly had it not been for the fact that soon after parts of the President's itinerary had become public, the discovery was made that some members of the Waffen SS were buried at a military cemetery in Bitburg which the President was scheduled to visit. A violent storm of protest immediately broke out in our country and in much of the Western world against the President's participating in a ceremony that could be interpreted as honoring Hitler's elite troops—soldiers who had led the atrocities against millions of Jews as well as others whom the Nazis marked for extermination. Here at home, war veterans of every faith, leaders of the Jewish community, churchmen, members of Congress, journalists—all joined in urgent, at times tearful, appeals that the President drop the Bitburg visit.

In view of my responsibilities in Bonn, I of necessity had a part in this unfolding drama. It was as clear to me as to many others that the original decision to go to Bitburg was ill-conceived. I thoroughly understood and respected the feelings of moral outrage of the distinguished citizens who pleaded with the President to reconsider. But I also knew what some critics either did not know or did not understand sufficiently.

The German Chancellor, Helmut Kohl, is among the staunchest friends the United States has anywhere in the world. He was the architect as well as the manager of the President's visit. His political prestige was committed to it. Had he relieved the President of the commitment to go to Bitburg, his power to govern would certainly have been weakened and could have been destroyed. His political opponents were already charging him with bungling and being an American lackey. Moreover, while there were many Germans who doubted the wisdom of the Bitburg visit, there were many more who were puzzled or resentful of the pressure being put on the President not to go there. They did not feel about the Bitburg cemetery as did the more violent critics of the President outside their country. To be sure, the Germans of today generally despise the memory of Hitler's storm troopers; nevertheless, many could not overlook the fact that those buried at Bitburg were among their kith and kin, and that they along with ordinary soldiers died in defense of their country. Some who felt that way began to murmur that American Jews were exercising undue influence on world affairs, and a widely read German periodical actually published an unabashed antisemitic article on "Die Macht der Juden" (The Power of the Jews).

In these circumstances, it became clear to me that the American-German relationship would be seriously damaged if the President refrained from going to Bitburg, and that antisemitism would also be reawakened here and there. On the positive side, I felt that America's reputation in Germany as well as elsewhere in the world required that our President remain true to his pledged word, and that it served American interests to have the Germans as well as other peoples abroad accept President Reagan as a steadfast leader whose devotion to international harmony was strong enough to overcome massive domestic pressures. I therefore never wavered in supporting the President's decision to go to Bitburg. The soundness of this judgment was later confirmed by the upsurge of good will among the German people toward the United States that was released by the President's visit. And in our country and elsewhere the furor about Bitburg soon died down—in part, I like to think, because of calmer understanding of the complex circumstances surrounding the President's visit.

I have dwelt at some length on the Bitburg affair because it contains an important lesson for all of us. What I learned from it, and what I believe everyone should learn from it, is that the reconciliation between the German public and other peoples of the world is less complete than was generally supposed. Unhealed wounds remain a painful legacy of the Nazi era; "Shadows of the evil past"—as Helmut Schmidt put it— are still haunting us, and many years of sensitive moral and political education will be required before we Americans, the Germans, and other peoples reach the mutual understanding and the indestructible friendship to which a troubled world aspires.

We cannot expect our German friends, especially those born during the past half-century, to live with a sense of personal guilt on account of the Nazi crimes; and we certainly should avoid subjecting every German action to a special test of moral purity. Nevertheless, there is no way for the German nation to escape the historical burden of responsibility for the Holocaust. The German people cannot both be proud of Beethoven and forget Hitler's crimes against humanity.

Reflections on Germany and Its Future

Even before the President's German visit my wife and I were already involved in farewell meetings with German colleagues, friends, and well-wishers. On some of these occasions we were asked our impressions of Germany. In responding, we expressed our admiration for the country and its people—for the beauty of the German landscape, the splendor of the medieval churches and castles, the cleanliness of the cities and villages, the charm of their winding streets and half-timbered dwellings, the courtesy and friendliness of the German people, their fondness for the fine arts, their absorbing interest in music, their gift for lively conversation, but above all—their firm and practically universal commitment to democracy and the rule of law. Once or twice, when asked what shortcomings we found in Germany, my wife, after thinking a while, noted the inability of people to do any shopping, even for groceries, in the evenings or on weekends. When my turn came, I was less reticent, but I too left no doubt that I shared my wife's warm admiration for Germany.

I left Germany more confident about its future than I was when I first came there. West Germany has become a democracy whose citizens respect and appreciate human rights. We Americans had something to contribute to the building of the new Germany, and we can justly be proud of the spirit as well as the substance of our contribution. But the ethical and political renewal of Germany was chiefly accomplished by the generation of Germans that arose from the ashes of destruction left by a terrible war. They have by now erected for their children a democratic society based on the rule of law and individual freedom.

To be sure, the country continues to face serious problems. Its old capital, Berlin, is still an isolated and divided city, Germany is still a divided nation within a divided continent, the armaments race remains very worrisome to its people, and the extensive unemployment of recent years is still to be overcome in West Germany. Nevertheless, German anxiety, while never absent, is less intense than it was four or five years ago. West Germany's firm adherence to NATO's double-track decision, its agreement to the deployment of modernized nuclear weapons on its territory, ended a long period of uncertainty and political turmoil. Demonstrations in the streets still take place, but they attract far smaller numbers and occur less frequently. The strength of the recovery from the recent recession has thus far disappointed many, but the longer-range economic outlook is gradually improving. A start has been made toward breaking the bonds that block constructive economic change. In particular, the government budget is being put in order, inflationary forces are being successfully curbed, market forces are being given somewhat freer rein, and there is increasing support for relieving the crushing burden that taxes on incomes and on business transactions have placed on individuals and corporations.

Most encouraging of all is the more wholesome behavior of young people. University students these days are again devoting themselves primarily to their studies rather than to demonstrating in the streets. They appear to be thinking constructively about their careers—an attitude I did not detect several years ago. A better understanding of their nation's tragic history is gradually emerging among them. Here and there, pride in their nation's achievements in science, literature, music, and the fine arts is beginning to return. Hope, that most fundamental of all economic forces, is beginning to blossom in the generation that will assume political and economic leadership fifteen or twenty years from now. Thus, by and large, I see reasons for confidence that Germany will tackle its problems resourcefully and that it will remain a constructive member of the Western community of nations.

TWO

The Economic Sluggishness of Western Europe

During my sojourn in Germany I had ample opportunity to ponder the economic sluggishness that has become characteristic of that country, and practically all of Western Europe, in the past ten to fifteen years. This sluggishness has been likened to a debilitating disease and is often referred to as "Eurosclerosis." Today I would like to describe some of its manifestations, discuss its causes, and indicate why I believe Americans have a deep stake in a full European recovery.

Emergence of Economic Sluggishness

The onset of European economic sluggishness can be traced to the early 1970s, but during much of that decade it was not obvious that the economic problems of Europe differed in kind from the problems of the United States, Japan, or other industrialized nations. In all these countries the preceding quarter-century was marked by extraordinarily rapid economic growth and relatively low inflation. The nations of Western Europe shared fully in that performance; indeed, during the 1960s growth rates in most of these countries, Britain being a notable exception, exceeded those in the United States.

This happy era was followed by the stagflation of the

19

1970s—slower growth accompanied by rapid inflation. Specific patterns of economic behavior of course differed from country to country, but during much of the 1970s it was easy to view those differences as variations on a single stagflationary theme. As time passed, however, that view became increasingly untenable, and today it is clear that Europe's problems are of a special kind.

The early 1980s were marked by a worldwide recession, brought on in part by governmental efforts to subdue an accelerating inflation. When I arrived in Germany in mid-1981 the question that dominated German economic discussion was whether or when an economic recovery would take place. That concern, while entirely understandable, missed the main problem facing the economy. After all, a business recession always releases corrective forces which sooner or later—whether or not governmental policies come to their aid—generate an economic revival. The main problem then facing Germany was not whether or how soon the downswing of its business cycle would be succeeded by an upswing. The basic question was—and still is, despite the recovery that began in 1983—whether the economy of Germany, along with those of the other countries of Western Europe, could regain the rapid upward thrust that had marked the 1950s and 1960s and thus become able once again to create abundant job opportunities for individuals who are able to work and seek to do so.

German citizens, along with other Europeans who have visited the United States in the past few years, often come back with tales of wonder at the vitality and dynamism of the American economy. There is ample reason for their spirited reaction to the American scene. Since November 1982, when our recession reached its lowest point, over 9 million jobs have been added in our country. In Germany and most of Western Europe, on the other hand, employment has changed little despite the recent pickup in over-all production. And the contrast between our country and Western Europe becomes still more striking when we take a longer view. Between 1970 and 1985 the number of gainfully employed individuals increased by over 28 million in the United States, while it hardly budged in Western Europe. At present, despite the current recovery, over 10 percent of the labor force of the European Economic Community remains unemployed. In Germany the unemployment rate is below 10 percent; in Britain, Belgium, and the Netherlands it is well above that figure.

Role of Welfare Programs

The economic difficulties of Western Europe during the early 1980s did not stem merely from business recession. In fact, the recession then under way was superimposed on a protracted weakness in the underlying forces of economic growth. This erosion of economic dynamism had many causes. Important among them were the two oil shocks of the 1970s, which exacerbated inflation and checked economic growth in the entire international economy. But the major factor that weakened the European economy did not derive from any foreign source; it originated within Europe itself.

Social welfare programs, which had gradually expanded in Western Europe during the immediate postwar decades, took a sharp upward spurt after 1970. They eventually embraced, besides old-age pensions and unemployment insurance, a wide range of programs dealing with sickness, disability, occupational safety, vocational guidance, child care, maternity care, housing and other vicissitudes of life. The scope of the welfare state did not stop with such individual or family concerns. It also came to include special benefits to business firms or industries that happened to be ailing or that otherwise were deemed worthy of encouragement. The more prominent of these benefits consisted of price supports for farm products and subsidies or tax concessions for businesses, besides protection through tariffs or quotas against foreign competition.

This flowering of the welfare state brought many blessings to Europe's increasingly impersonal and industrialized society; it certainly contributed to social and political stability. But when the welfare state is carried to excessive lengths, it can weaken a nation's economy. That is precisely what happened in West Germany and pretty much throughout Western Europe. In Germany, government spending already constituted about 38 percent of its gross national product in 1970—a figure that slightly exceeds the American level even now. By 1982, the enormous expansion of the welfare state brought government spending to 50 percent of the gross national product. A similar explosion of outlays on welfare programs occurred throughout Western Europe. At present, government spending is a little below 50 percent of the gross national product in some countries, as in Britain; in others, as in The Netherlands and Sweden, it is above 60 percent.

Not surprisingly, the expansion of the welfare state through governmental largesse has been accompanied in Europe by profound changes in labor markets. Trade unions benefited from governmental solicitude, became increasingly powerful, and drove up wages sharply toward the end of the 1960s in practically every West European country. Wages continued to rise faster than the cost of living during the 1970s despite a declining tendency in productivity gains. Moreover, the costs of employee benefits borne by employers kept rising; of late they have amounted to a little under 40 percent of direct wages in the United Kingdom, over 70 percent in West Germany, and over 80 percent in Italy and France.

Government regulations designed to consolidate the welfare state added further to business costs and reduced the ability of business firms to respond to changing market conditions. In Germany and many other countries of Western Europe it has become difficult and expensive to discharge employees even when they are no longer needed. Establishing a new business in Germany may require up to 150 approvals; moving a plant to a new location may entail obtaining several hundred permits; selling by retail shops has for many years been forbidden during evenings and on weekends. In France it often takes two years to incorporate a business. In Italy, until very recently, a business firm could secure new workers only from registers maintained by the Ministry of Labor.

The vast "social safety net" created in Germany and elsewhere in Western Europe naturally led to sharp increases in the taxes imposed on business firms as well as in their labor costs and regulatory burdens. Labor markets became more rigid. In Germany annual wage adjustments became nearly uniform for all enterprises across the country—in firms large or small, those successful or unsuccessful. As a consequence, it became "more difficult for employers in expanding industries to bid up wages to attract labor, or for laid-off workers in declining industries to bid down wages to get their jobs back." The inevitable result of higher costs and higher taxes was a deterioration of business profits. The average rate of profits in German enterprises reached a peak around 1965 and moved along a horizontal path until 1970; the trend since then, apart from cyclical recoveries such as the one now under way, has been downward. During the 1970s the trend of profits was much the same throughout Western Europe. The incentive for undertaking new business capital investments thus tended to shrink along with the wherewithal for financing them.

The proliferation of welfare programs also had an injurious effect on work discipline, and this too had an adverse influence on economic performance. To meet the high costs of managing the welfare state, heavy taxes could not be confined to well-to-do individuals and business firms. High taxes on employees inevitably followed. Meanwhile, generous benefits to the unemployed, students, and low-income groups assured those who did not work, or who worked only lackadaisically, an income that often was not much lower than the earnings of diligent members of the labor force. These developments diminished the incentive to work for many individuals, and they apparently lured an increasing number into the "shadow economy." Needless to add, the short work week, long vacations, frequent holidays, liberal sick leaves, provisions for cures, and early retirements did not improve over-all economic performance. At present, the normal number of workhours per year in Western Europe is well below that in the United States and far below that in Japan; and it appears to be lower in West Germany than anywhere else in Europe.

The rapid expansion of the welfare state after 1970 thus became a dominant force in the economic malaise of Western Europe. Labor's share in national income rose substantially and that of investors kept shrinking. Annual increases in capital investment by business firms became generally smaller. A large part of the capital investment that took place in Germany was directed at reducing the need for overpriced labor; productivity gains benefited from the substitution of capital for labor, but still slowed down. Declining rates of economic growth became general in Europe. Governmental budget deficits accompanied growing tax burdens. Unemployment rose along with the rate of inflation, although some countries— notably, Germany and Switzerland—still managed to keep inflation under decent control. And while the rate of inflation has slowed down in most parts of Europe since 1980, unemployment still appears to be increasing in Western Europe taken as a whole.

Contrasts between Europe and the United States

Our own country too has escaped neither the benefits nor the burdens of the welfare state. As the programs of the Great Society initiated in the 1960s unfolded, many of the symptoms of the European malaise appeared also in our midst. We escaped, however, the European excesses of the welfare state.

Social welfare programs in our country were not carried nearly as far as in Europe. To be sure, unemployment and inflation also marked the American scene; but our trade unions never attained the power exercised by their European counterparts, and our governmental benefits for the unemployed remained relatively restricted, both in amount and duration. The level of real wages in the United States was virtually stable during the 1970s; and while unemployment tended to rise, it remained preponderantly of short duration, and therefore was less serious than the long-term unemployment that afflicted Europe.

We also were spared the inefficiency of nationalized industrial enterprises as well as government monopolies in the transportation, communications, and public utility fields—all of which have plagued European economies. Moreover, the over-all tax burden in our country rose little during the 1970s, while it climbed rapidly in Europe and reached levels far exceeding ours. The tax burden on our corporations actually declined, and—more important still—the rate of return on invested capital stayed well above European levels.

The spirit of risk-taking and entrepreneurship therefore remained alive in the United States. During the 1950s, when I worked on economic problems with President Eisenhower, one of our deep concerns was the loss of jobs in New England, particularly in Massachusetts. Numerous textile firms were moving to the Carolinas and elsewhere in the South; leather and shoe factories were closing; shipbuilding was in the doldrums. In these circumstances, it seemed proper for the federal government to undertake measures for relieving local unemployment, but efforts made in that direction proved ineffective. Meanwhile, a revival of the Massachusetts economy gradually got under way and in time gathered momentum. This was not a result of any systematic plan, but a response to the opportunity that private citizens accustomed to risk-taking recognized in their environment—particularly, the existence of relatively low wages, a large pool of professional skills, an abundance of venture capital, and a concentration of scientific and engineering talent in the major universities of their region.

Entrepreneurially-minded scientists joined venture capitalists, enterprising commercial bankers, and managerial experts in establishing and nourishing hundreds of small high-technology firms. Before many years passed, they succeeded in transforming Massachusetts into one of the most progressive parts of our nation's economy. What happened along Route 128 outside Boston during recent years has occurred in greater or lesser degree in other areas of our country where universities and scientific institutes flourish—most dramatically, in the Silicon Valley of California. To be sure, various new commercial ventures had their intellectual and technological roots in governmentally financed research, but this was an unplanned and indirect result of governmental activity.

Many of the newly founded firms became involved in developing sophisticated computers, microelectronics, telecommunications, office automation, genetic engineering, biomedicine, and other marvels of modern technology. Besides the new jobs that were directly provided by the high-technology firms, myriad jobs were created in supporting service trades. These trades benefited also from improvements in the general standard of living, the expanding refinements of urban life, and the spin-off of activities previously performed in traditional industries and households. Our national economy thus became to an increasing degree a "service economy" dominated by small and medium-sized firms. As a matter of fact, about 8 million Americans outside of agriculture are now self-employed; their numbers have been increasing faster than the working population as a whole.

Large firms are obviously essential in some of our key industries, as in the production of steel, automobiles, and electricity; but there are numerous trades and industries in which small businesses have distinct advantages over large firms.

Small businesses are subject to lower rates of taxation; they are burdened less by government regulation; they are able to avoid the unwieldiness of large corporations in reacting to new market conditions; they can operate with shades drawn in contrast to the glass-house environment of large businesses; and they can usually manage their affairs without being encumbered by restrictive work rules imposed by trade unions. At present, none of the Silicon Valley firms is unionized, and I believe that much the same is true of other high-technology centers.

These objective factors would, however, have been of little avail had it not been for the entrepreneurial spirit itself—the adventurous attitude of mind that drives some men and women to seek self-fulfillment through their independent efforts. By starting a business of their own, ambitious and self-assured individuals could escape the stifling atmosphere that envelops so many of our large corporations, and be their own masters as they struggled to create a new way of life, if not also a fortune, for themselves and their families. The number of such individuals has apparently been increasing in our country.

There has been no corresponding upsurge of entrepreneurship in Europe. To be sure, many European firms have an outstanding record in turning out precision machinery, in producing chemical and pharmaceutical products, in telecommunications, and other modern industries. High-technology centers, however, are few and of limited scope; in West Germany they are virtually confined to Stuttgart and Munich. On the other hand, traditional industries—such as coal mining, steel, textiles, and shipbuilding—are a significantly larger factor in European economies than in our own; but these are the very industries that of late have exhibited the greatest weakness. And while the service trades are expanding in Europe as well as here, they have not yet reached the prominence that they have attained in our country.

There are many reasons why the entrepreneurial spirit is

less firmly implanted in Europe than in the United States. I have already alluded to some of them: the high level of taxation, the regulatory burdens, the immense power of trade unions, and the increasing share of labor in national income. There are also other inhibiting factors in Europe. Venture capital firms are few in number and very limited in their resources. Capital formation by way of stock offerings is practically unknown. Preferential tax treatment of corporate capital gains—which could bring forth a flood of venture capital, as happened in our country since 1978—is neglected. And European markets for industrial products remain fragmented despite the vaunted "common market" of the European Economic Community.

The institutional limitations on entrepreneurship are reinforced by inhibiting psychological attitudes. In Europe workers are less willing than in our country to move from one place to another or from one branch of industry to another. Investors there are more fearful of failure and therefore less inclined to take risks. Commercial bankers tend to concentrate on financing the expansion or rationalization of on-going concerns. Venture capital firms are likewise cautious and tend to confine themselves to aiding firms that have already begun to demonstrate growth potential. Educated men and women tend to value public service and job security more than the challenge of establishing a business of their own. Universities tend to stay aloof from the business world. Scientists who choose to work in private industry are commonly viewed with some disdain by their university colleagues. There are, of course, many exceptions to these generalizations. But there can be no doubt that Europeans are much less inclined to take business risks than are Americans, and that this is significant among the reasons why Western Europe has been so deficient during the past ten to fifteen years in creating new jobs.

When the focus of comparison is shifted from the United States to Eastern Asia, the shortcomings that have marked the European economy in recent times become more glaring. The people of the free-enterprise countries in that part of the world—namely, Japan, South Korea, Taiwan, Hong Kong, Singapore, Thailand—are still accustomed to hard work. With the exception of Japan, they know little about social welfare benefits. Taxes have been relatively low, trade unions have been weak, business profits have tended to be high, new industries have been thriving, job opportunities have been increasing, and the standard of living has kept rising. This, indeed, is the region where economic incentives have propelled economic growth to a faster rate during the past decade than is found anywhere else in the world. To be sure, the growth of the free-enterprise area of Eastern Asia has slowed sharply in the past year; but this appears to be a temporary setback, caused in large part by weakness in the rest of the international economy. The competitive power of Eastern Asia in world markets has become and will remain a major challenge to the West, especially to the industrial nations of Western Europe.

Uncertainties Surrounding the Future

How well the nations of Europe will respond to the economic challenge of other countries, including our own, is a matter of considerable uncertainty. The structure of security that Europe has built around individuals and business firms has seriously reduced the power of the market to create jobs and rapid economic growth. The recovery now under way, while very welcome, is a cyclical development. There is no justification as yet for regarding it as the beginning of a long-run rejuvenation of the economy of Western Europe. If Europe's earlier economic dynamism is to be regained, Europeans will have to curtail the excesses to which their welfare state has been carried.

But the remedy of stripping away the excesses of the welfare state is not easy to apply, as the conservative governments now in power in Great Britain, Germany, our own country, and elsewhere have discovered. Just as people are inclined to focus on the benefits and to ignore the costs when social programs are adopted or extended, so are they inclined to focus on what they would lose and to ignore what they would gain when cutbacks are proposed. And just as special interests often have the power to override the national interest by securing governmental favors, so are they often able to override the national interest when it is proposed to curtail these favors. It is an inescapable fact that Europeans, or for that matter people in the industrial democracies generally, have come to regard the welfare benefits they are accorded by their governments as their natural right—as something to which they are unreservedly entitled, and which therefore cannot justly be removed or even appreciably reduced.

If the people of Western Europe cling stubbornly in the years ahead to their security blankets, the malaise of their national economies will not be cured and may in fact deepen. But I do not believe this will happen. The reason for some optimism is that Europeans are becoming increasingly aware of the connection between the excesses of the welfare state and the persistent sluggishness of their economies. The startling contrast between their circumstances and those of the more dynamic economies of the United States and Eastern Asia has led to agonized introspection and a flood of studies and proposals by academicians, private research organizations, and government agencies. This intensive self-examination is beginning to bear fruit.

Let me mention some recent developments. The German government, having made good progress in slowing the growth of its outlays and in reducing its budget deficit, has just put into effect a tax reduction of moderate size and has committed itself to a further reduction in 1988. Britain, and to a lesser extent Italy and Germany, have been "privatizing" some of the government's equity in industry and closing down some outmoded industrial facilities. Italy has weakened the automaticity of cost-of-living increases in wages. France has moderated upward adjustments in the minimum wage. Germany has extended from six to eighteen months the period for which employers can hire workers without a commitment to retain them. France, Germany, and The Netherlands have increased the incentive of workers to find jobs by reducing unemployment benefits to some degree. In Britain those benefits have become subject to the income tax; Britain has also made it easier for employers to hire non-union workers. Most countries in Western Europe have taken steps toward deregulation of financial markets, thus opening up new and more efficient routes for the flow of savings to businesses that can put them to work. Moreover, possibilities that were unthinkable a short time ago, such as permitting Saturday work and relaxing the government's monopoly of telecommunications, are now being seriously considered in Germany.

Despite these constructive changes in European thought and action—and the list could be lengthened considerably—it would be premature to conclude that Europe is firmly on the road to full recovery from its protracted economic sluggishness. The reforms that have taken place fall considerably short of the declared intention of governments. Nowhere has the scope of the welfare state been appreciably diminished. Even relatively minor changes in social welfare programs have often been bitterly contested by the affected parties. In short, what has thus far been achieved amounts to only a small part of what needs to be done to restore economic dynamism in Western Europe.

While all that and more can be said by way of criticism, it is important to recognize that easy money has been largely avoided in Europe since 1980 and so too has loose governmental finance. The main exception has been France, but its reversion in 1981 to Keynesian and Marxist therapy proved disastrous and had to be abandoned. Sound governmental finance is thus again being generally practiced in Western

The rate of inflation has been successfully subdued in
countries, and it has already been brought to a vir-
ᴜal halt in Germany. These are noteworthy stepping stones
to a rejuvenated West European economy. With the good
sense of the European democracies reasserting itself, there is a
basis for hoping that majorities of European citizens will before long recognize the wisdom of cutting back substantially
on the lavish indulgences that the welfare state has brought
into being.

Importance of European Economy to the United States

Just how distant that day may be is a matter of great importance to the United States. The countries of Western
Europe have long been major trading partners of ours; we
share a common history and culture with them, and they are
our military and political allies. If Europe can regain its earlier
economic dynamism, our foreign trade and financial dealings
will benefit; the adequacy of Europe's contribution to our
common defense burden will be reasonably assured; strains
in the NATO alliance will tend to diminish; and the outlook
for international peace will brighten. On the other hand, if the
trends that I have reviewed should persist, Western Europe
may face a Spenglerian future—a future of economic stagna-
tion, if not actual decline. Such an unhappy development
would also darken the economic and political future of our
own country.

It is, therefore, clearly to our national interest, as well as
that of Europe, that American leaders in government, business, science, and finance aid Europe's recovery by any
means available. Perhaps the most important assistance our
country can give is to continue offering an example of a better
way—a way that effectively combines the compassionate cor-
rection of unacceptable market outcomes with the preserva-

tion of the market's power to meet material needs in an ever more abundant fashion. The worst thing we can do for Europeans—and ourselves—is to overlook the lesson they are painfully learning about the excesses of governmental intervention in the economy. There is a threat of this kind in the rising tide of protectionist sentiment in our country and our Congress. But my faith in the ultimate wisdom of democracies extends to the United States as well as Europe.

THREE

The Future of German-American Relations

A few years ago we celebrated the 300th anniversary of the arrival on our shores of the first immigrants from Germany. The thirteen Mennonite and Quaker families who in 1683 settled in Germantown, now a part of the city of Philadelphia, came in search of freedom—the freedom to pursue their religious beliefs and the freedom to seek economic betterment. They found both. I dare say that a great majority of the forebears of the approximately 60 million Americans who today claim German ancestry came in search of the same objectives—personal freedom and economic opportunity.

These people, their children, and their children's children forged the chain that linked our two societies. These links had little to do with political treaties, security arrangements, or trade agreements. Indeed, they survived severe strains in the political relationship between our countries—even two terrible wars. The durability of these human ties is attested by the speed and commitment with which so many of our people devoted themselves to assisting the German people after World War II. Among the belligerents in that tragic conflict, Americans were the first to extend once again a hand of friendship to the Germans.

It was primarily the good will of our people and the interaction between them and the German people that brought democracy and reconstruction to the Federal Republic of Germany and established the partnership between our two societies that exists today. To be sure, the Marshall Plan was a vital element in rebuilding West Germany's shattered economy. The North Atlantic Treaty provided the essential guarantee of security against aggression. Other actions, such as the Berlin airlift, further showed the resolve of the United States to share in the protection of the young democracy that had risen from the ashes of World War II. But the driving force of all these constructive developments was the network of human relationships created by the millions of Americans of German descent, the multitude of Germans who found refuge in our midst during the 1930s, the hundreds of thousands of German war prisoners who lived for years in our country, the legion of scholars and exchange students and countless other Americans and Germans who cooperated in shaping the democratic society which the Federal Republic is now. It was their interaction that formed the foundation of the partnership between our two countries—a partnership that has proved capable of withstanding all sorts of economic irritations and political differences.

Past Irritations and Differences

There have been many of both during the past forty years. There was, for example, the American proposal during the 1960s for a multilateral naval force, which after prolonged discussion with Germans and other Europeans was finally shelved by President Johnson. Later, Henry Kissinger's call for a "new Atlantic Charter," which it was hoped would crown 1973 as the "Year of Europe," stirred opposition among our allies, found German support wanting, and came to little in the end. Much more troublesome were the vacillating American ideas in the late 1970s concerning the "neutron bomb." The very possibility of its deployment on German soil caused massive anxiety—especially among politicians of the left, school teachers, ecologists, clergymen, and youngsters. The furor subsided after President Carter decided not to proceed with the "bomb"; but this decision disappointed the German government and left a residue of hard feeling for a time. Many of us will have little difficulty recalling the more recent controversies—the forceful American objections to the Siberian natural gas pipeline; the widespread protests and demonstrations of many German citizens against the deployment of Pershing II's and cruise missiles; the American concerns over some European—including German—foreign trade policies; the German complaints about our high interest rates and our awesome federal deficit; the American displeasure over the inadequacy of German support of our policy toward El Salvador and Nicaragua; the German complaints— and the much louder ones from other Europeans—about American reluctance to intervene in foreign exchange markets; the American pressure on the German government to take stronger measures to invigorate its economy so that it could play a larger role in the restoration of international economic order; the continuing anxiety of many Germans— including some high government officials—over implications for their country of the "strategic defense initiative" that President Reagan unveiled in March 1983, and so on and on.

Some of these recent irritations—particularly the two most serious ones, namely, the controversies over the Siberian pipeline and over the deployment of modernized nuclear weapons—have by now been resolved. Others, such as the recurring differences over defense burden-sharing and the disputes over trading in steel and agricultural products, have been partially accommodated. At times, regrettably, there have been excesses of political and journalistic rhetoric on both sides of the Atlantic, and there have been some misguided actions as well. Nevertheless, the United States and the Federal Republic have generally succeeded in working out, or at least in muting, their differences. Not only that, but a cooperative spirit has marked the workaday relations between the bureaucracies of our governments, our respective military forces, and the business, financial, and cultural communities of our two countries—a dimension of international life that receives little public notice.

This ability to work together and to practice mutual accommodation even when governments and underlying conditions in our two countries kept changing is a fact of great significance; for it indicates that the interests that unite us—social, political, economic, and military—are strong enough to overcome even divisive issues. That at any rate has proved to be the case thus far, and from that we can draw some encouragement for the future.

Sources of Future Differences

We will doubtless continue to have differences with our German ally. Indeed, they may become more frequent and more acute than in the past. Having become more affluent and more conscious of their ability to influence the course of events, the Germans are nowadays more inclined to assert their independence and to pursue with skill and vigor what they consider to be their national interest.

Ways of dealing with the Soviet Union will remain a source of tension between our countries, for we view the Soviets rather differently. To West Germans, the Russians appear brutal, bent on expanding their already vast political power, and hardly trustworthy. Nevertheless, Germans feel deeply that they must learn to live with their dangerous neighbor—both in their own interest and that of their compatriots in East Germany whom the Soviets hold hostage. Regardless of which political party may be in power, Germans therefore put great store on trade as a vehicle of détente and are reluctant to link economic transactions to Soviet behavior. We, in contrast, are much more inclined to mix economics and politics. We see the Soviets as our political, military, and ideological rival around the globe. We are less hesitant in denouncing their repression of human rights or in imposing economic sanctions to punish their foreign aggressions. We trust the Soviets even less than do the Germans and are therefore more cautious about entering into agreements with them.

Second, the divergence of our other international interests is likewise bound to cause occasional strains in the German-American relationship, just as it has in the past. The concerns of the Federal Republic are centered most of all on East Germany, but to a large degree also on its allies in the European Community. We, on the other hand, besides being deeply involved in East-West relations, have large interests around most of the world—Latin America, the Near East, the Pacific area, and Africa. The Germans want us to devote more of our attention to Europe; we in turn want the Germans to become more involved outside of Europe, particularly in the Persian Gulf area. We thus tug at one another's elbows, each trying to turn the other in unwelcome directions.

In the third place, our economic attitudes and interests are not identical with those of West Germany. Most Germans believe in an elaborate welfare state and approve of rather close governmental regulation of the economy. We, in contrast, are less committed to extensive social welfare programs and are inclined to accord much larger scope to private enterprise. More serious than these philosophic differences are our divergent attitudes toward some financial and trade issues, such as the sharing of defense costs and trading with the Soviets and their satellites as well as between ourselves. More recently, participation in research findings and the transfer of technology have become highly controversial issues and could be the source of major strains in the future.

Instead of becoming exercised over these or other sources of tension, we should regard them as the entirely normal agenda of the relationship with our German ally. Nations that are separated by geography, language, and culture, and whose interests are not identical in all respects, can hardly avoid having and articulating their differences. We need not fear to confront our differences with West Germany. On the contrary, we need to understand and deal with them responsibly if NATO is to survive and remain robust.

German Sentiments Toward America

In considering the future of German-American relations, we dare not assume that because we have gotten along well during the past forty years we will continue to get along well in the future. It is true that the German people preponderantly mistrust the Soviet Union just as they did a generation or two ago, that a great majority of them continue to recognize the need for NATO to deter Soviet aggression, and that most Germans continue to think well of the United States. Still, German attitudes today are not the same as they were immediately after the war, or even during the 1950s and 1960s. Their confidence in American leadership of the West and in our willingness to come to the defense of Germany in the event of war is no longer as great or as widespread as it was a generation ago. Anxiety over the rivalry between the Soviet Union and the United States has intensified among Germans, and so too has the wish to avoid involvement in it. Fear of nuclear war between the superpowers, which could turn all Germany into a graveyard, has encouraged neutralist inclinations. These attitudes are confined to a small minority, but they appear to be spreading, especially among young people.

Neither time nor my knowledge will permit adequate tracing of the causes of these shifts in German sentiments. Some of the contributing factors are, nevertheless, quite evident. One is a loosening of the network of human relationships that previously had closely linked our societies. By the late 1960s and early 1970s the creative generation of Germans and Americans who had cooperated in the political and economic reconstruction of Germany was no longer dominant in positions of leadership and influence. Their successors have had no similar formative experiences. Their familiarity with CARE packages, the Marshall Plan, and the Berlin Airlift, or even with the repression by the Soviets of East Germans in 1953, of Hungarians in 1956, and of Czechoslovak citizens in 1968 is, at best, indirect and cloudy. Little burdened by historical knowledge, the new generation has been reacting—as people do generally—to the experiences of their own time. Some developments involving our country—the Vietnam War, the Watergate crisis, the occasional belligerent rhetoric of our national leaders, as well as the gains of Soviet military power and influence around the world—have all served to deprive the United States of the luster of its earlier moral and heroic image.

While we may regret the shift in German sentiments toward the United States, we should regard it as the emergence of a more traditional relationship between independent countries. The task now facing us is to find appropriate ways and means of preserving and, if at all possible, strengthening the bonds of friendship and cooperation that exist between our two countries.

Obstacles to Close Cooperation

We face obstacles in working toward this goal. One, which in fact underlies some of the difficulties on which I have already commented, is that the American political system is less predictable in the realm of foreign affairs than the parliamentary system of Germany or of other Western democracies. Our Presidents not infrequently bring to their high office little intimate knowledge or skill in the field of foreign affairs. At times, that is true even of our high officials in governmental agencies concerned with international affairs. Partly for these reasons, partly because of the exigencies of domestic politics, sudden shifts in our foreign policy are often feared and resented by other countries. European governments, in contrast to ours, are typically headed by a prime minister or chancellor who, by virtue of having served in parliament for many years, brings to his office considerable knowledge of foreign affairs as well as experience in working with the bureaucracy steeped in that area. That of itself tends to impart a somewhat greater element of stability and predictability to the foreign policy of parliamentary democracies than exists in our case.

There is another significant difference between our political system and that of other Western democracies, including Germany. Ours is a government of divided powers. To be sure, the President—acting directly or through one of his appointees—can enter into agreements with foreign countries; but his power to do that is often restricted by Congressional legislation, and, in any event, whatever agreements he reaches with foreign countries must still win approval in the Congress, either through explicit consent in the Senate or through the pursestrings controlled by both houses of Congress. But Congressional approval can be very difficult to achieve, as Woodrow Wilson, Jimmy Carter, and even Ronald Reagan have learned to their sorrow. European democracies do not suffer from any such handicap. There the legislative and executive functions are joined, and tight party discipline—something we lack—helps to assure parliamentary support of the government in power.

These differences in political systems will probably continue to cause irritation among Germans from time to time. Speaking realistically, about all that we can do about this is to strive for a bipartisan foreign policy and for greater continuity of service from one administration to another by some of the major political officers in our State and Defense Departments. Early success in these directions would be beneficial to us and to others, but it is also unlikely. It would therefore be well for our German and other foreign friends to stop complaining about our form of government and to recognize more fully the fundamental elements of continuity that do characterize our foreign policy.

There is a second factor that underlies the occasional tensions between us and our NATO allies—most of all with the Federal Republic of Germany. No amount of gentle rhetoric about equality in the German-American partnership can obscure the fact that the partnership is inherently unequal, and that as a practical matter it will continue to be so viewed by both the governments and the peoples of our two countries. The area of the United States is vastly larger than West Germany's; our population and economy are several times as large; our military power is incomparably larger; and our political influence in the world is correspondingly greater. These differences in size and power are beyond dispute; they are practically unalterable; they undoubtedly evoke a sense of security among the German people; but they also cause or intensify psychological attitudes that tend to strain the relations between our countries.

Helmut Schmidt, the former Chancellor of West Germany and a devoted friend of the United States, has articulated these psychological problems with exceptional clarity in his recent book, *A Grand Strategy for the West*. Let me quote a few passages:

> It is difficult for most Americans to visualize the situation of West Germany. First of all, it is difficult to understand the enormous psychological wounds that the division of Germany has caused—and the wounds are not healing. . . . West Germany is a small country, about the size of . . . Oregon or Colorado. But in Oregon or Colorado there are two or three million people. In West Germany there are sixty million. On top of that dense population there are, of course, military forces . . . our own forces numbering 500,000 soldiers . . . also the American forces, about 200,000, and French forces, British forces, Dutch and Belgian forces, Canadian forces, and even a Danish general. All of these are under a foreign high command.
>
> Think also of the foreign high commander having some 5,000 nuclear weapons within his command and not under the host nation's control . . . There is no other country in the

world that has such a concentration of military weapons and military power from seven nations on its soil—and all of it under someone else's command.

The foreign commander is, of course, an American general, subject to the authority of the American President, who alone has control over the nuclear trigger.

Although a great majority of the German people continue to value NATO and America's commitment to German security, that feeling is by no means universal. Even many who welcome America's military umbrella are apt to have mixed feelings, being troubled now and then by the limited sovereignty of their country, resenting their dependence on the good will of the American people, hoping that it can be counted on to continue, and yet wondering whether or how it might be safely terminated. These are natural human feelings; they are often expressed by young Germans, perhaps more often just harbored semi-consciously by both the young and the old.

Remoteness of European Political Union

In theory, there could be an effective way of reducing, if not actually overcoming, the psychological burden of dependency borne by the German people—namely, to have their country join its sister nations of Western Europe in transforming the present European Community into a full-fledged political union. In fact, many German and other European statesmen have worked ardently in the postwar years in behalf of a United States of Europe. Some are still doing it; and they are currently, as in the past, being encouraged by our government. Over twenty years ago, President Kennedy stated in a memorable address in Germany: "We look forward to a united Europe in our Atlantic partnership—an entity of interdependent parts, sharing equally both burdens and decisions, and linked together in the tasks of defense as well as the arts of peace . . . With only such a Europe can we have a full give-and-take between equals, an equal sharing of responsibilities, and an equal level of sacrifice." These sentiments have recently been reaffirmed by President Reagan.

A European political union would bring great advantages to the United States as well as to our NATO allies. Doing away with frontier posts in Western Europe; eliminating divergent national standards with regard to health, safety, and the environment; ending governmental procurement policies that favor indigenous enterprises; establishing a common currency and tax system—these and other rearrangements following from political union would create a large integrated "common market" in Western Europe, make possible extensive economies of scale, release beneficial forces of competition, and generate new jobs and new wealth all around. Political union would also strengthen the self-assurance and the self-reliance of Europeans, especially in West Germany where feelings of dependency are most acute. In such a political environment, the European contribution to our common defense would almost certainly be appreciably larger, and the United States could by common consent gradually withdraw a significant part of the military forces that are now committed to Europe. Moreover, dealing with a single powerful European partner would probably enable us to arrive at common policies more speedily and to better effect than dealing with the numerous partners we now have in NATO—each of limited strength, some pulling in one direction and others in another

Unhappily, recent Community meetings in Milan and Luxembourg have demonstrated that nationalistic sentiments in Europe are still too strong to make political union possible in the reckonable future. That will occur, if at all, only by small steps in a gradual process. But the advantages of a truly integrated common market are so clear that it would be surprising if some constructive steps in that direction did not take place over the next decade. Political union is a much more remote possibility. However, a few preliminary steps toward such a goal—among them, the creation of a modest European monetary system and the direct election of a symbolic European Parliament—were taken during the late 1970s, and others are now being actively discussed. Hence, further steps toward unified political action, while far short of outright political union, may well occur before the end of this century. The key to substantial progress lies in a closer working relationship between France and Germany, as both President Mitterrand and Chancellor Kohl fully recognize. The United States should therefore use every opportunity to help move these two allies, and perhaps later also others of the European Community, toward building institutions that promote closer political consensus. Just as the renewal during the past few years of America's confidence in itself has made us a stronger ally of Western Europe, so too would a more unified and more confident Western Europe make Germany and our other European partners stronger allies of the United States.

Paths to Minimizing Tensions

Given time, other steps that are perhaps less difficult of attainment can contribute to tranquility in German-American relations. Let me mention a few: First, the discomfort felt by many Germans over the continuing presence of American and other foreign troops on their soil could be allayed by stationing a German brigade or two on American soil. Such a move would have no military value since German and Allied soldiers are now concentrated where the military threat is greatest. It could, however, have psychological significance by symbolizing the military unity and political interdependence of our countries. If the United States initiated such a move, other NATO allies might follow. Military symbolism could thus help Germans feel that in our troubled world their soldiers have a role in other countries just as American and other Alliance soldiers have a role in Germany.

Second, both Americans and Germans need to recognize that despite the close relationship between our countries, we have not yet achieved the full confidence that we should have in one another. Americans need to understand better the mood of a divided nation—a country cut off from its roots, still trying to find its identity. Germans need to understand better the massive commitment of the United States to human freedom and world peace. Both of us must respect to a greater degree one another's special interests. Americans should leave no doubt about our support of the constant efforts of West Germany to build closer ties between the families, business entities, and cultural institutions of the two Germanys. West Germany in turn should be more fully aware of the problems our country faces in Central America and lend larger support to our efforts to stabilize that sensitive area.

Third, better consultative procedures between us and our German and other allies are needed in the interest of NATO harmony. President Nixon's recent comment that "we have sometimes treated the Europeans as poor relations who were expected to follow us meekly down any path we chose" is less true today than it was ten or twenty years ago. We surely have been consulting extensively with our allies, and most of all with the Germans, about the negotiating positions on arms control that we have been advancing in recent years in Geneva. The German government has been our full partner— at times more than a full partner—in these complex negotiations. But we have not yet developed the habit of consulting with our NATO allies frequently enough or thoroughly enough on the broad range of economic and political issues that are of common concern. And even in the security area, we slipped badly when we announced to the world the "strategic defense initiative"—a matter that profoundly affects the security interests of our allies—without consulting or even informing them in advance.

I must add, however, that consultation needs to be a two-way street. The Germans would do well to keep us better informed about their ongoing relations with the East Germans—perhaps also with the Poles and others in the East. Consultation must also not be allowed to become a vehicle for achieving harmony at the cost of shirking fundamental principles. The nuclear threshold will not be lowered unless our European allies finally decide to achieve a full conventional defense, and we must never tire of reminding them of this essential requirement of military stability.

Fourth, and most important of all for the long run, is the need on the part of the peoples of our two countries to regain the kind of understanding that enriched our partnership in the first decade or two after the war. The educational system, which could have partially replaced the loss of direct personal experience between Germans and Americans, has failed us. German textbooks give little or no attention to the vast changes that have occurred in our society since 1945; they even neglect the contemporary history of their own country. American textbooks rarely discuss domestic affairs or developments in Germany, so that students are denied the opportunity to learn about the nature of German society. Besides these shortcomings of historical education, American schools have become deficient in the teaching of foreign languages, and the schools of both our countries have served the new generation poorly by their slight attention to the principles that inform our Western civilization. These shortcomings of our schools need to be addressed not only by professional educators, but also by clergymen, journalists, politicians, and—most of all—by the parents of our children.

If I am right in thinking that understanding between democratic governments depends fundamentally on the kind of relationship that exists between their peoples, it is highly important that improvements in the educational systems of the United States and the Federal Republic be supplemented by a larger network of personal contacts between our peoples. The goal of our two countries should be to bring about widespread understanding of our respective institutions of work and play, of life in our homes and communities, and of the aspirations and concerns of our citizens. There is no better way of regaining some of the spirit of camaraderie that existed between Germans and Americans in the early postwar years—a camaraderie that forged the partnership between our governments in furthering peace and protecting freedom.

Fortunately, a significant increase in youth "exchanges" has taken place in the past few years, the most noteworthy being a program under which every member of Congress and of the Bundestag has the opportunity to nominate a teenager from his or her electoral district to spend a school year in the partner country. This and other youth exchange programs need sensitive nurturing by responsible citizens. We also need to develop much further our adult exchange programs—those involving scientists, working youth, middle managers of business firms, journalists, and legislators, besides professional educators. Greater attention to improving and enlarging the contacts between Germans and Americans is something we owe to ourselves and to those who will follow in our footsteps.

Importance of Germany to the United States

In the course of this lecture, I have referred repeatedly to the close ties between the German and the American people. We Americans are bound by history with strong moral, political, and economic ties to the German people. West Germany is also our security partner—indeed, is the linchpin of the Atlantic Alliance. It alone commits its entire military force—and it is a sizable and highly skilled force—to NATO. Its economic and financial prowess exceeds that of every other country in Western Europe. If the United States, as is sometimes urged, were to withdraw its military forces from the European continent, Germany and probably the rest of Western Europe would have no choice but to accommodate its foreign policy to that of the neighboring superpower, the Soviet Union. The balance of power, both economic and political, would then shift drastically against our country—if not at once, surely over time. To protect our security, we would need to become a Fortress America: our military budgets would soar, the standard of living of our people would decline, and some of the freedoms that we treasure would probably diminish as well. We clearly need Germany and the rest of Western Europe, just as they need us.

About the Author

Arthur F. Burns was United States Ambassador to the Federal Republic of Germany from May 1981 to June 1985.

In a long and distinguished public career he has also served as Chairman of the Board of Governors of the Federal Reserve System (1970–78); President and Chairman of the National Bureau of Economic Research (1957–68); and Chairman of the President's Council of Economic Advisers (1953–56).

Ambassador Burns, who received his Ph.D. from Columbia University in 1934, was a member of the economics faculties of both Rutgers (1927–43) and Columbia (1941–69) Universities. He is currently Distinguished Scholar in Residence, American Enterprise Institute for Public Research.

His principal publications include: *Production Trends in the United States since 1870* (1934); *Measuring Business Cycles* (with W.C. Mitchell) (1946); *Economic Research and the Keynesian Thinking of Our Times* (1946); *Frontiers of Economic Knowledge* (1954); *Prosperity Without Inflation* (1957); *The Management of Prosperity* (1966); *Full Employment, Guideposts, and Economic Stability* (with Paul A. Samuelson) (1967); *The Defense Sector and the American Economy* (with Jacob K. Javits and Charles J. Hitch) (1968); *The Business Cycle in a Changing World* (1969); and *Reflections of an Economic Policy Maker* (1978).

Arthur Burns was born in Austria in 1904.

Recent Publications of the Council on Foreign Relations

Strategies for African Development, Robert J. Berg and Jennifer Seymour Whitaker, editors, in cooperation with the Overseas Development Council, University of California Press, 1986.

The United States and Germany: A Vital Partnership, Arthur F. Burns, Council on Foreign Relations, 1986.

East Bank/West Bank: Jordan and the Prospects for Peace, Arthur R. Day, Council on Foreign Relations, 1986.

The Conventional Defense of Europe: New Technologies and New Strategies, Andrew J. Pierre, editor, Council on Foreign Relations, 1986.

Blocking the Spread of Nuclear Weapons: American and European Perspectives, in cooperation with the Centre for European Policy Studies, Council on Foreign Relations, 1986.

A Widening Atlantic? Domestic Change & Foreign Policy, Ralf Dahrendorf and Theodore C. Sorensen, Council on Foreign Relations, 1986.

Trade Talks: America Better Listen!, C. Michael Aho and Jonathan David Aronson, Council on Foreign Relations, 1985.

Compact for African Development, Committee on African Development Strategies, Council on Foreign Relations in conjunction with the Overseas Development Council, 1985.

Latin Migration North: The Problem for U.S. Foreign Policy, Michael S. Teitelbaum, Council on Foreign Relations, 1985.

Third World Instability: Central America As A European-American Issue, Andrew J. Pierre, editor, Council on Foreign Relations, 1985.

India and the United States, Council on Foreign Relations, 1985.

Ripe for Resolution: Conflict and Intervention in Africa, I. William Zartman, Oxford University Press, 1985.

Arms and the African: The Military Influences on Africa's International Relations, William J. Foltz and Henry S. Bienen, eds., Yale University Press, 1985.

For complete catalog and ordering information please contact Publications Office, Council on Foreign Relations, 58 East 68th Street, New York, N.Y., 10021 (212) 734-0400.